# What to Do When FRIENDS Are BULLIES

**Addy Ferguson**

**PowerKiDS** press™

New York

Published in 2015 by The Rosen Publishing Group, Inc.
29 East 21st Street, New York, NY 10010

First Edition

Editor: Jennifer Way
Book Design: Erica Clendening and Colleen Bialecki
Book Layout: Andrew Povolny
Photo Research: Katie Stryker

Photo Credits: Cover Image Source/Getty Images; p. 5 manley099/E+/Getty Images; p. 6 LWA/The Image Bank/Getty Images; p. 7 greenland/Shutterstock.com; p. 9 funstock/Thinkstock; p. 10 Christopher Futcher/E+/Getty Images; p. 11 Craig Dingle/E+/Getty Images; p. 13 Uwe Krejci/Digital Vision/Getty Images; p. 14 PhotoAlto/PhotoAlto Agency RF Collections/Getty Images; pp. 15, 20 Monkeybusinessimages/Thinkstock; pp. 17, 19 Jamie Grill/Iconica/Getty Images; p. 18 KidStock/Blend Images/Getty Images; p. 21 Rob Marmion/Shutterstock.com; p. 22 Comstock Images/Stockbyte/Thinkstock.

Library of Congress Cataloging-in-Publication Data

Ferguson, Addy.
 What to do when your friends are bullies / by Addy Ferguson. — 1st ed.
    pages cm — (Stand up: bullying prevention)
 Includes index.
 ISBN 978-1-4777-6877-8 (library binding) — ISBN 978-1-4777-6878-5 (pbk.) — ISBN 978-1-4777-6619-4 (6-pack)
 1. Bullying—Juvenile literature. 2. Peer pressure—Juvenile literature. I. Title.
 BF637.B85F472 2015
 302.34'3—dc23

                              2013046669

Manufactured in the United States of America

CPSIA Compliance Information: Batch #W14PK5: For Further Information contact Rosen Publishing, New York, New York at 1-800-237-9932

# ontents

What Is Bullying? ............................................. 4
Different Ways to Bully ..................................... 6
Peer Pressure and Bullying ............................... 8
The Effects of Bullying ................................... 10
Don't Be a Bystander! ..................................... 12
How to Be an Ally ........................................... 14
Buddy Up ....................................................... 16
Talk to an Adult ............................................. 18
A Bully-Free Zone ........................................... 20
No One Deserves to Be Bullied ......................... 22
Glossary ........................................................ 23
Index ............................................................ 24
Websites ....................................................... 24

# What Is Bullying?

Do you know what a bully is? A bully is a person who hurts another person over and over again. Often the person being picked on has less power than the bully. This could be either because she is not as strong as the bully or because she may not seem to fit in with other kids. The person being picked on is called the **victim**.

You may **witness** bullying around you. You may not know the bully or the victim. Other times, though, you may know the bully and the victim. What do you do if you realize that your friend is the bully?

You may have seen a bully hurting someone at your school. This book will tell you things you can do if one of your friends is being a bully.

# Different Ways to Bully

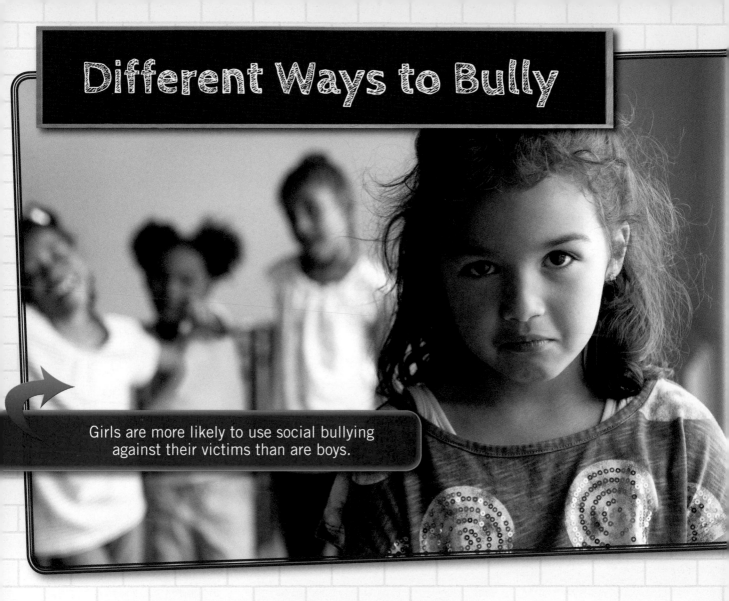

Girls are more likely to use social bullying against their victims than are boys.

You may think all bullies are alike. There are many different ways that kids bully one another. Some bullies push, shove, hit, or otherwise **physically** hurt their victims. This is called physical bullying.

Other bullies, called **cyberbullies**, use technology to bully. They use texts, emails, social networking sites, and other online tools to spread rumors and hurt others' feelings. There are also social bullies, who get other people to **exclude** a target. Verbal bullies use words to hurt. No matter what kind of bully you think your friend might be, one thing is certain. Bullying is wrong.

When you think of bullying, physical bullying might be what you picture in your head. There are other ways that bullies hurt others, though.

# Peer Pressure and Bullying

Is your friend using you and your other friends to help bully his victim? When a group of people puts pressure on another person to encourage him to do something he would not normally do, this is called **peer pressure**.

You may not feel that you can say no to a friend who wants you to be mean to another kid. You might be afraid your friend will then turn on you or you will lose your other friends. However, if you do what you know is right, you will feel better. You might even see that once one person says no to peer pressure, others will, too.

You can use peer pressure to do good things. For example, you and your friends could tell your bullying friend that you won't join him in bullying because it is wrong. Your friend might then feel peer pressure to stop bullying.

# Don't Be a Bystander!

The people who see someone being bullied without taking part in it are called bystanders. Bystanders may feel that by doing nothing, they are not doing anything wrong. Letting a bad thing happen to someone else is wrong, though. By watching and not saying anything, bystanders make it seem like they think bullying is OK. This gives children who bully power.

If your friend is bullying someone, do not be a bystander! Don't give in to peer pressure by joining in or keeping quiet. Talk to your friend and let him know you do not like how he is treating people.

Bystanders have power, too. They can tell the bully to stop. This can be hard to do, but it might make your friend stop and think about what he is doing.

# How to Be an Ally

Another way to stop your friend from bullying another person is to try to help the person being bullied. Invite that person to play at recess or to sit with you at lunch. Bullies often target kids who are loners. If you start being friendly to the kid being bullied, your friend might stop bullying her.

Walking home with the kid who is being bullied will help him feel safer.

Talk to your friend about the person she is bullying. If your friend starts to see her target as a person with similar interests, she might not be as quick to bully her.

You can also be an **ally** by helping the child being bullied avoid the bully. This could mean something as simple as walking home with him.

# Buddy Up

You may have other friends in your group who do not like the behavior of your bullying friend. Buddy up with them to discourage your friend from bullying. Bullies often bully to feel powerful. When people just look on and say nothing, the bully feels like nobody can stop him.

If you team up with some friends to tell a bully to stop, you take away the bully's power. You and your friends can also do this by inviting the kid being bullied to hang out with you. This will make it harder for your friend to single out that kid to bully her. You will also give the bullied kid a boost to her self-esteem.

Standing together as a group to stop a friend's bullying is easier than trying to do it by yourself.

# Talk to an Adult

If you are not sure what to do about your friend's bullying, sometimes the best thing to do is to talk to an adult. You might be afraid that your bullying friend will be punished for his behavior, but getting an adult involved is sometimes the best way to start making things right. Talking to a trusted person about your feelings will help you feel better, too.

A parent, grandparent, teacher, the school counselor, or even an older sibling may have ideas on how to deal with bullying. Asking for advice is a good idea.

Being bullied is stressful. Encourage the kid being bullied to talk to someone about her feelings and to ask for help to stop the bullying.

Encourage the child who has been targeted to talk to an adult or trusted person, too. Having someone to talk to can go a long way toward getting rid of the feelings of loneliness, sadness, anger, and shame that come with being bullied.

# A Bully-Free Zone

Antibullying clubs are groups that raise awareness about bullying. They also work with teachers and principals to make their schools bully-free zones.

Many schools are working hard to put a stop to bullying. They are working to create bully-free zones. This means that everyone, including the principal, teachers, and the students, promises to watch for bullying and stand up for the victims.

Creating a bully-free zone takes a lot of work. The entire school community has to do its part. If you think your school is up to the challenge, you can talk to your principal or a teacher about starting an antibullying program or club. It can all start with just one person who is willing to stand up to bullying.

A school community that strives to be a bully-free zone is saying that it does not accept that bullying is a normal part of growing up.

BULLYING

# No One Deserves to Be Bullied

Even if it is hard to stand up to a friend, remind yourself that nobody deserves to be bullied. You may be afraid to lose your friendship, but hopefully your friend will realize you are trying to help.

If your friend needs someone to talk to in order to help him stop bullying, you can offer to go with him to the school guidance counselor or another adult. Even if he has been a bully, it does not mean you cannot help him learn to be a better friend to everyone.

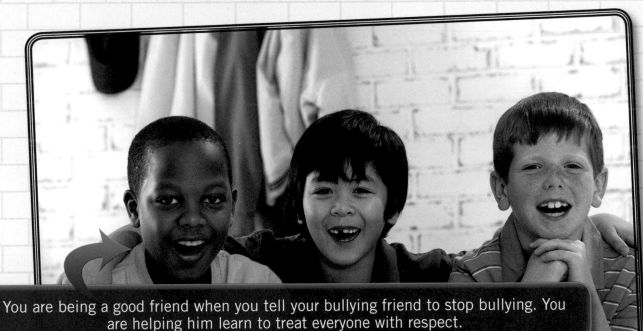

You are being a good friend when you tell your bullying friend to stop bullying. You are helping him learn to treat everyone with respect.

# Glossary

**ally** (A-ly)  A person or group that helps another person or group.

**cyberbullies** (SY-ber-bu-leez)  People who do hurtful or threatening things to other people using the Internet.

**depression** (dih-PREH-shun)  A sickness in which a person is very sad for a long time.

**exclude** (eks-KLOOD)  To keep someone out or shut out.

**peer pressure** (PEER PREH-shur)  When friends or classmates make you feel like you have to do something you do not want to do.

**physically** (FIH-zih-kul-ee)  Having to do with the body.

**self-esteem** (self-uh-STEEM)  Happiness with oneself.

**victim** (VIK-tim)  A person or an animal that is harmed or killed.

**witness** (WIT-nes)  To watch an action or event.

# Index

**B**
behavior, 11,
      16, 18

**E**
emails, 7

**F**
feelings, 7, 18–19

**G**
group, 8, 16

**L**
loneliness, 19
loners, 14

**P**
power, 4, 12, 16

**R**
rumors, 7

**S**
sadness, 19

self-esteem, 10–
      11, 16
shame, 19
social networking
      sites, 7

**T**
technology, 7

**V**
victim(s), 4, 6, 8
      11, 20

# Websites

Due to the changing nature of Internet links, PowerKids Press has developed an online list of websites related to the subject of this book. This site is updated regularly. Please use this link to access the list: www.powerkidslinks.com/subp/frnds/